Silkie Chickens

by Julie Murray

FANCY FARM ANIMALS

Abdo Kids Jumbo is an Imprint of Abdo Kids
abdobooks.com

abdobooks.com

Published by Abdo Kids, a division of ABDO, P.O. Box 398166, Minneapolis, Minnesota 55439. Copyright © 2026 by Abdo Consulting Group, Inc. International copyrights reserved in all countries. No part of this book may be reproduced in any form without written permission from the publisher. Abdo Kids Jumbo™ is a trademark and logo of Abdo Kids.

Printed in the United States of America, North Mankato, Minnesota.

052025

092025

Photo Credits: Adobe Stock, Getty Images, Shutterstock

Production Contributors: Teddy Borth, Jennie Forsberg, Grace Hansen
Design Contributors: Candice Keimig, Pakou Moua

Library of Congress Control Number: 2024947621

Publisher's Cataloging-in-Publication Data

Names: Murray, Julie, author.

Title: Silkie chickens / by Julie Murray

Description: Minneapolis, Minnesota : Abdo Kids, 2026 | Series: Fancy farm animals | Includes online resources and index.

Identifiers: ISBN 9798384905264 (lib. bdg.) | ISBN 9798384905967 (ebook) | ISBN 9798384906315 (Read-to-me ebook)

Subjects: LCSH: Chickens--Juvenile literature. | Birds--Juvenile literature. | Farm animals--Juvenile literature. | Livestock--Juvenile literature. | Domestic animals--Juvenile literature.

Classification: DDC 636.52--dc23

Table of Contents

Silkie Chickens 4

Body 10

Diet 18

Baby Silkie Chickens 20

More Facts 22

Glossary 23

Index 24

Abdo Kids Code 24

Silkie Chickens

Silkie chickens are known for their soft, fluffy feathers. They are also gentle, friendly, and cute. All these **traits** make them excellent fancy farm animals!

Silkie chickens **originated** in Asia. Most people believe they came from China or Japan. Silkie chickens traveled west on the **Silk Route**. They were brought to the United States in the mid-1800s.

Most Silkie chickens live on farms. They are raised for their eggs. The eggs are small and delicious. Silkie chickens are also kept as house pets.

Body

Silkies are smaller-sized chickens. They often look bigger because of their fluffy feathers. Males can weigh up to 4 pounds (1.8 kg). Females are a bit smaller.

Silkies' beautiful feathers cover their head, body, and legs. The feathers can be many colors. Some are black, white, **buff**, or blue.

While most chickens have four toes, Silkies have five toes. They also have bluish earlobes. These special features can be hard to see through their feathers.

Silkie chickens have a large, puffy **crest** on the top of their head. They also have a walnut-shaped **comb** that is brown or purple in color.

Diet

Silkies mainly eat chicken feed. This gives them all the **nutrients** they need. They also eat greens such as kale and lettuce.

19

Baby Silkie Chickens

Female Silkie chickens lay up to 10 eggs at a time. The eggs hatch after about 20 days. The chicks are tiny when they hatch. Silkies can live for about 8 years.

More Facts

- Silkies have bluish-black skin and bones. They have **wattles** that can be hard to see through their feathers.

- A hen will lay about 120 eggs each year.

- Female Silkies are good and caring mothers. They will even hatch and raise the young of ducks and other chickens.

Glossary

buff – a yellowish-brown color.

comb – the fleshy part on the heads of some birds.

crest – a tuft of feathers on an animal's head.

nutrients – something in food that helps people, animals, and plants live and grow.

originate – to start.

Silk Route – a network of trade routes that connected Asia to Europe and the Mediterranean.

trait – a feature that makes an animal different from others.

wattle – the fleshy and often brightly-colored folds of skin under the necks of certain birds.

Index

babies 20
body 10, 12, 14
China 6
coloring 12, 14, 16
comb 16
crest 16

eggs 8, 20
feathers 4, 10, 12, 14
food 18
head 12, 14, 16
Japan 6
legs 12

origins 6
personality 4
size 10
traits 4
United States 6
uses 8

Visit **abdokids.com** to access crafts, games, videos, and more!

Use Abdo Kids code **FSK5264** or scan this QR code!